GLOBAL MENTAL HEALTH
A GLOBAL LOOK AT DEPRESSION

CONNOR WHITELEY

Copyright © 2019 Connor Whiteley

All rights reserved.

DEDICATION

Thank you to all my readers because without you I couldn't do what I love.
Thank you to Mrs. Shepley for introducing me to psychology

INTRODUCTION
Depression, mental health, physical sickness.

All are real.

These things and many more affect all of us, even if we realise it or not.

However, all countries, all people, all societies show symptoms of disorders or sicknesses in different ways- and that is as a result of one major factor... culture.

Our culture; a set of beliefs, attuites and values belonging to a group of people; is a powerful thing.

As our culture provides us with many vital aspects of ourselves that we ultimate take for granted.

For example, our culture shapes our:

- Values- what we hold dear and what we stand for.
- Attudtidies- a set way of thinking. Such as homosexuality is okay or *'normal'*
- Beliefs- what we believe to be right or wrong.

When I wrote 'normal' earlier, I wasn't trying to be discriminatory, but I would like to highlight something that will be featured in this book, and that is that normality is a construct, and nothing is normal.

As normality is merely what society has created for it's through creating a set of social norms, so people know how to behave and what is excepted from them.

Furthermore, it the idea of culture and the differences between them that will take centre stage in this book.

As together we travel around the globe examining how culture impacts people's beliefs around mental health as well as depression.

So, please join me on this journey as we travel the world exploring this interesting idea of culture impact depression.

For knowledge is worth sharing…

CHAPTER 1: DIAGNOSIS OF MENTAL HEALTH CONDITIONS

Firstly, I would like to apologise to any readers that have already read my Abnormal Psychology as this chapter and the three afterwards will be taken from the book. As a way to introduce people to how depression is diagnosed and caused.

Firstly, we'll look at what is abnormality?

Think about it, what does abnormality mean to you?

There are several theories that we'll look at now.

Abnormality as A Deviation From Social Norms:

This theory states the abnormality is something that isn't 'acceptable' in society.

While this is a good common-sense approach and the approach that I personally use but a limitation of this theory is that social norms change over time.

For example, homosexuality was classified as a mental disorder and wasn't classed as a social norm until it was legalised in the UK in 1967. Only then could this behaviour be classed as normal.

Abnormality as inadequate functioning:

This theory belongs to Rosenhan and Seligman (1989) and it proposes 7 criteria that can be used to define abnormality.

Those 7 are:

- Suffering
- Maladaptive (for instance: not being able to achieve life goals)
- Unconventional behaviour (behaviour than not a lot of people do)
- Unpredictable behaviour
- Being irrational (so you can't understand why they behave that well)
- Observer discomfort (it makes you uncomfortable to watch the behaviour)
- Violation of moral standard

A strength is that the theory embraces more dimensions of what abnormality is. Such as socially acceptable behaviour causes suffering to the person.

A weakness is that very few disorders meet all 7

criteria, so are they not abnormal behaviour?

Abnormality as A Deviation From Ideal Mental Health:

This theory was proposed by Jahoda (1958) and for her theory, she used the idea of ideal health. Therefore, she thought that it was more important to define what health is than abnormal behaviour.

She proposed the following as indicators of ideal mental health:

- Voluntary control of behaviour
- You have to have positive relationships
- You need to be productive.
- You need to have an accurate perception of the world.
- You need to have efficient self-perception.
- You need to have realistic self-esteem.

A strength is that the theory is more humanistic as it focuses on health over disorders.

Although, as not many people would meet all six then is everyone not entirely healthy.

Classification Systems:

A classification system is a diagnostic manual providing a set of symptoms, a system of diagnostic categories (the type of disorder) as well as rules for making a diagnosis on these set of symptoms.

China uses its own manual called: the Chinese Classification of Mental Disorder (CCMD-3) and it's widely used by some other countries as well.

The World Health Organisation uses the International Classification of Diseases (ICD-10) and it's used in many European countries. Before an edition is published it has to be approved by all WHO members.

Finally, the USA and other countries use the Diagnostic and Statistical Manual (DSM-5) It's published by the American Psychiatric Association.

Biases in Diagnosis:

However, there are many biases that affect diagnosis. For example:

- The sick role bias- when a doctor looks for something wrong with the patient because the patient came to them so there must be something wrong.

- Confirmation bias- where doctors look for evidence to confirm their suspicions than evidence that doesn't.

And there is much, much more that can affect the reliability of diagnosis. But to drench your thirst for more here are two studies that show how unreliable diagnosis can be and a study showing the role of culture in diagnosis.

Rosenhan (1973):

8 mentally healthy people tried to get admission to a mental hospital.

In the interview, the patients said that they were hearing voices saying empty, hollow and thug. Apart from this, they told the truth about everything.

Upon admission, they acted normally and wanted to be discharged from the hospital.

They secretly took note of their observations.

Results showed that seven of the 8 were admitted and were diagnosed with schizophrenia.

Took on average of 19 days for the patients to get out of the hospital via own means.

When discharged their schizophrenia was in remission.

None of the hospital staff thought they were healthy patients.

Normal behaviour was interrupted as symptoms of a disease.

In conclusion, psychiatrists lack the ability to tell the difference between a sane person and a disorder.

Critically Thinking:

A strength of the study is that the experiment was completed at a number of US hospitals so the results can be applied potentially to the whole country.

On the other hand, the study lacks temporal validity because the study was done back in the 1970s and since then our knowledge of disorders has improved, so the results probably wouldn't apply now.

Le-Repac (1980):

5 white and 4 Chinese American therapists were compared to see when shown a video of white and Chinese patients would their conclusions be the same.

They were tested on their definition of abnormality, empathetic ability and perception of the patient.

Results showed both cultures agreed on the

concept of abnormality.

Americans were more accurate when predicting self-descriptive responses.

Americans thought Chinese patients were depressed and less socially poised.

Chinese thought Americans to be more disturbed.

Differences were down to therapists' own biases and world views.

Critically Thinking:

The study has strong internal validity; does the study measure what it intends to; because it shows that culture can affect a clinician's judgement.

However, the study doesn't use two distinctly different cultures as both were American in whole or part. So, is it possible that the results would show a bigger or smaller gap of difference between other cultures?

CHAPTER 2: BIOLOGICAL CAUSES OF DEPRESSION

Now, we're starting to get to what I call proper psychology and my favourite parts of psychology because to this and the next two chapters are some of the most interesting pieces of psychology.

As we start to explore the why and the reasons behind why Major Depressive Disorder develops.

Firstly, we are starting with a biological basis for MDD.

There are two theories for why MDD develops within the biological world. The first is called the serotonin hypothesis.

This theory states that MDD is caused by an imbalance of serotonin in the brain. Serotonin is a neurotransmitter associated with many functions in the body and it's sometimes referred to as the happiness chemical. As it's associated with happiness as well as well-being.

Source: *https://www.medicalnewstoday.com/kc/serotonin-facts-232248*

There are two pieces of evidence supporting this hypothesis:

- Supported by: certain drugs known to decrease serotonin are known to have depressive side effects.
- Drugs that increase serotonin levels can relieve depression symptoms. Like: Selective Serotonin Reuptake Inhibitors (SSRIs)

However, a major criticism and a problem that I personally have with this theory are that once you take an SSRI the level of serotonin in your blood increases within an hour. However, depressive symptoms don't decrease until a month later.

Therefore, it begs the question: is it actually the increase in serotonin that cures your depression? Or does that increase start another bodily process and that process takes a month to finish and that process cures your depression?

I know that it sounds strange or not thought out but if the serotonin hypothesis is true, then surely your depression could be cured within an hour of you taking the SSRI as within that hour the serotonin imbalance is gone or reduced?

<u>The Neurogenesis Hypothesis:</u>

On the other hand, modern research has been focusing on the Neurogenesis theory of depression. The theory states that depression is the result of a lack of neuron birth in the hippocampus (this is the part of the brain responsible for emotion) and in other places in the brain that is related to serotonin, dopamine and norepinephrine.

In addition, cortisol appears to be the reason for this lack of neurogenesis. (the birth of neurons in the brain) Patients with MDD show a symptom called HPA-axis hyperactivity. This results in the over-secretion of cortisol. (too much cortisol is being released) This leads to reduced levels of serotonin as well as other neurotransmitters in the brain, including dopamine. This has been linked to depression. Demonstrating how complex the brain's chemistry is, and why the treatment for depression remains problematic. As we will explore later.

There are a few pieces of evidence that support this theory as well.

- Depressed people tend to have smaller hippocampi than the rest of the general population.
- Stress hormones are increased in MDD patients and this appears to stop neurogenesis in the hippocampus, as shown in rodents and other primates.
- Finally, anti-depressants can increase neurogenesis in the hippocampus in rodents.

Source: https://www.thinkib.net/psychology/page/22460/biological-approach-to-depression

Supporting Studies:

Caspi et al (2003):

The 5-HTT gene is responsible or the production of serotonin.

A longitudinal study of 1,037 children from New Zealand. Divided into three groups: people with two short alleles of the 5-HTT gene, one long and short alleles, two long alleles.

They were assessed from the age of 3 to 25.

A life history calendar was used to assess stressful life events.

Subjects were assessed for depression with an interview and information from someone who knew them well.

A GUIDE TO MENTAL HEALTH AND TREATMENT AROUND THE WORLD

Results showed that there were no differences in the number of stressful life events.

People with two short alleles managed life events with more depressive symptoms.

Critically Thinking:

The study effective looks at the genetic argument for the serotonin hypothesis.

Nonetheless, this study does have ethical concerns. For example, the distress that knowing that you're genetically more likely to develop depression.

Therefore, the costs and benefits of research must always be calculated before the research is done.

Kendler et al (2006):

Over 42,000 twins were recruited for the study across a 60-year age span for the purpose of generational comparison.

They used a computer-assisted telephone interview that was conducted using DSM-4 criteria for MDD.

Informed consent was got before the interview. Trained interviewers were used with a lot of medical training to collect data.

The aim was to reach both pairs within a month.

Results showed prior studies got similar results. Heritability of depression is 38% on average.

Didn't differ very much across the generations.

No evidence was found that the shared environment was a factor in developing depression.

In conclusion, major depression is moderately inherited.

<u>Critically thinking</u>:

The study is highly reliability as a number of studies have supported its findings that depression is about 37% inherited.

However, this study is open to population fallacy; were your sample does actually represent the general population; because most of the population aren't twins.

CHAPTER 3: COGNITIVE CAUSES OF DEPRESSION

Moving to our next point of interest is how can our mental processes affect our chance of developing MDD.

Now the main theory of depression used for this type of explanation is: Beck (1967) and the theory states that cognition (mental processes) is the main reason behind depression and focuses on the impact that a change in automatic thoughts can have on behaviour. The theory focuses on:

- The cognitive triad- negative beliefs about the self, the world and the future. These influence the automatic thoughts to be pessimistic.
- Negative schema- the negative beliefs about themselves become generalize and people start to think negatively about everything that happens to them.
- Faulty thinking patterns- people think and make illogical conclusions because of how they process information is biased.

Personally, I do quite like the theory because if you know someone with depression as I did then you can see some of this theory out to light.

In addition, I think that it's a reasonably easy theory to follow.

But let's put this theory into context, according to this theory a depression is caused by:

(I know some the examples are poor)

- The cognitive triad- this can be demonstrated when a depressed person says things. Like: "I'm useless," or "Oh the world is falling apart so what's the point of living?"
- Negative schemas- as demonstrated by this: "Oh I failed in art so I'm never to pass any subjects, go to university and I'm just going to be a failure in life,"
- Faulty thinking patterns- this could be shown in a setting when researching a holiday to the most beautiful place ever and there was a 0.5% chance of a terror attack. "Oh no, I can't go there I'm going to die,"

While that last example wasn't the best. It shows how illogical conclusions can be made because of a bias towards the negative.

A GUIDE TO MENTAL HEALTH AND TREATMENT AROUND THE WORLD

Supporting studies:

This first study shows how having a negative thinking style can affect depression.

Alloy, Abramson and Francis (1999):

Quasi-experiment and longitudinal study for 5.5 years with a questionnaire and structured interviews.

Freshmen were given a questionnaire to determine their cognitive style and they were split into two groups based on the results.

High risk; the negative cognitive style; believed that negative life events were cataphoric and the results meant that they were flawed and worthless.

During the first 2.5 years, high-risk people were more likely to develop symptoms of major depression. (17% versus 1%)

High-risk people were more likely to have suicidal thoughts and behaviour (28% versus 13%)

In conclusion, negative cognitive style can lead to the development of major depression.

Critically Thinking:

This study was a longitudinal study, so this allowed the researchers to show the effects of a negative thinking style over time.

Yet it was a quasi-experiment without a clear independent variable and the dependent variable, so it can't be said if the study has strong internal validity; does the study measure what it intended to; as it wasn't clear what the study was measuring.

Caseras et al (2007):

Quasi-experiment with eye-tracking technology

Using the Beck Depression Inventory, the subjects were assessed for depressive symptoms and then split into two groups. Depressed and non-depressed.

Then the subjects were shown 32 pictures paired with a positive, neutral and negative stimuli and each picture was shown for 3 seconds.

Using eye-tracking technology, the researchers measured what stimuli the subject first focused on and how long they focused on it before they switched to another stimulus.

Results showed that depressed people have an attention bias for the negative stimuli because once they looked at the negative stimuli, they found it hard to move onto another stimulus.

Critically Thinking:

The study used a large sample bias so the findings can be applied to large groups of people as we know that this trend of behaviour is shown by a number of people.

However, this is a reductionist way of thinking. A way of thinking that tries to find a single cause for depression without thinking of other factors and more holistic research that considers biological, cognitive and social factors of depression needs to be done.

CHAPTER 4: SOCIAL CAUSES OF DEPRESSION

Personally, this section is the least interesting for me because while I fully know that social factors DO play a role in depression and believe me I know.

I think that this section is really common sense about what social factors can cause depression and I prefer to learn and know the more theoretical content of psychology.

So as there's no theory to talk about. Let's quickly run through some factors that can probably cause depression.

These are the factors are Brown and Harris (1978) found that could increase the development of depression.

- Having 3 or more children
- Lack of intimate relationships
- Lack of employment

- Loss of mother

Supporting Studies:

Kivela et al (1996):

Quasi-experimental, longitudinal study

A study was completed in 1984-85 on depression of over 1,500 elderly Finnish people.

Those that were not depressed were interviewed and reassessed in a follow-up study in 1989-1990.

Through questionnaires, certain life events and social variables that occurred during 1984-1989 were assessed.

Depressed and non-depressed people were compared.

Results showed that in 1989-90 8.2% of men were depressed and 9.3% of women were depressed.

Powerful predictors for men were: poor relationship and negative change with Spouse, moving into intuitional care and loss of mother under twenty.

Powerful predictors for women were: loss of father under 20, low religious activity and worsening relationship with neighbours.

In conclusion, social factors and changes in social ties can be predictors in developing depression at old age.

Critically Thinking:

While the study effectively shows how elderly people can get depressed because of social factors. There is probably a lack of temporal validity; how valid the results are because of time; because Finland like the rest of the world has got through the cultural and social change since this experiment was done. Therefore, can the results still be valid considering this social change over time?

Unless the experiment is redone, we will not know.

Rosenquist, Fowler and Christakis (2011):

You will find this study interesting!

Statically analysis of social networks and longitudinal study.

Participants were taken from an earlier study in 1948 in Framingham and the researchers took information in order to keep track of these people in case they were needed again.

A questionnaire for depression was done three times between 1981-2001.

Rosenquist, Fowler and Christakis computerized

and analysed the data in 2011.

Results showed that people up to 3 degrees of separation could be affected because:

Subjects were 93% more likely to get depressive symptoms if they were in direct contact with a depressed person.

43% for two degrees

37% for three degrees

Critically Thinking:

The study is numbers based so the results have a good scientific basis to support.

But the data of this study is fairly old and because we live in an ever-changing and developing world. How do we know if the results are still valid? Is it possible the results are higher or lower in today's society with the increased use of social media and other factors?

The problem with social research is that it needs to be redone about every ten years because of the fact that we live in a changing world.

CHAPTER 5: CULTURAL PSYCHOTHERAPIES AND THE ROLE OF CULTURE IN THERAPY

Now that we understand how depression is caused, we can now start to think about how culture can impact treatment as in this chapter. We will begin to introduce the topic to you before we start to look at the cultural differences that exist in terms of views of mental health around the world as well as the differences factors that can cause depression, as the culture itself can create differences in the reasons for the development of depression.

Additionally, I will not be including a chapter on western attitudes and the impact of western culture on treatment because I'll be referring to western societies throughout the book.

Therefore, without further a due- let's begin.

Indigenous Psychotherapy:

In the treatment of depression, there are a few different ways of treating it. They are:

Antidepressants

Cognitive Behavioral Therapy

Other forms of Psychotherapy- including talk therapy

However, the idea of indigenous psychotherapy is that these types of therapies are embedded within a culture as well as they don't include anyone from outside the culture. In addition, these therapies are carried out by someone who is given permission to perform the therapy within the community.

Furthermore, indigenous healing brings together therapeutic beliefs and practices that are anchored into the culture that it's being performed in. such as reliance on family as well as community network and religious beliefs.

While originally this idea does seem a little strange from a western viewpoint as surely there is only one type of psychotherapy or a psychological way to treat depression and surely this idea of culture/ indigenous healing is nonsense?

If you think about it, it's no different to what we actually perform in the west, as western societies have their own version of indigenous healing as well, because in the west our methods of treating depression does bring together therapeutic beliefs and practices as well as the aspects of societies that are important to us.

In western society this includes:

Productivity- in the west we are encouraged to live productive lives and contribute to our family.

Focus on family- as the family is a focal point for support and in the west and the rest of the world it's empathised that we need to be there for our family and support it. Whether financially or with enough resources to support it.

Putting the above examples in the westernised context for depression treatment, Cognitive Behavioural Therapy (CBT) focuses on changing the automatic thoughts of the patient to become more positive so that people can become more productive and focus on the good of their family, and in therapy the focus on family is important in the recovery as it provides motivation for the patient to heal/ improve.

Overall, the idea of indigenous therapy isn't exclusive to other non-western cultures because western therapies are created in the same way.

Cross-cultural psychotherapy:

Another type of psychotherapy that is impacted by culture is cross-cultural psychotherapy. This is referred to as multicultural therapy as well. This type of therapy differs from indigenous therapy because in indigenous therapy it involves a person from inside the community to perform the therapy.

Whereas in cross-cultural therapy, the therapist is from a different culture than the patient, then the therapist adapts the treatment methods that have been shown to be effective to meet the cultural needs of the patient.

Cross-cultural psychotherapies tend to be performed after a disaster has happened and other countries sent in psychologists and therapists amongst other experts to help the country or affected people recover.

However, it's a great shame from western therapists don't adapt therapies for the new culture that they're trying to help as when I was first introduced to this topic back in 6th Form. We watched a video on how tribes in west Africa treated depression and there was a section in the video that had a village elder tell us about how strange and ridiculous the western treatment method was as you go into a dark room instead of being outside in the fresh air and in the west you don't have the entire village or community come out to support you.

A GUIDE TO MENTAL HEALTH AND TREATMENT AROUND THE WORLD

In the end, the village elders had to ask the therapists to leave because the therapists were being disrespectful to their culture and they were causing conflict.

Personally, I believe that it's a great shame that the western therapists were disrespectful and didn't culturally adapt their method of treatment for these people. As a lot more good could have come out of their visit if they had been respectful and listened to elders about their unique culture.

Furthermore, the therapists should have thought about the cultural impact of treatment in the following way: if the African therapists came over to the west to perform treatment with their idea of bringing everyone and performing the therapy in the open air. Then the African therapists would be disappointed as in western culture- we are all 'to' busy to stop our day and come together to support a friend or family member. Let alone a stranger. Therefore, the African therapist would need to adapt their treatment as well.

That's what the western therapists needed to do.

<u>Research and The Effectiveness Of Cultural Therapies:</u>

Indigenous therapies reflect the values as well as practices of a given culture.

However, the study of indigenous psychotherapy

is difficult for several reasons.

- Indigenous therapies require no formal training within families and communities and it's not open to outsiders.
- There's a lack of standardised procedures so it's very difficult to evaluate its effectiveness as there's little continuity in its procedures.

As a result of these and other factors, there's a lack of reliable studies that would provide results that would allow you to perform a meta-analysis so you could effectively get an average on the effectiveness of these indigenous therapies.

Nevertheless, there are exceptions to this problem that will be explored in the book as we start to investigate specific cultures.

Below are two case studies that demonstrate the effects of culture on treatment.

Kinize et al (1987):

Examined 41 depressed southeast Asian patients who were being treated with antidepressants in a US clinic.

Blood tests were run and it showed that 61% of patients were not taking the medication.

This is because of the social stigma that is

A GUIDE TO MENTAL HEALTH AND TREATMENT AROUND THE WORLD

associated with taking antidepressants.

Cultural attitudes about authority caused patients to pretend to compliance about treatment as a way to not offend the doctors.

However, after a doctor-patient discussion about the benefits and problems of antidepressants. Compliance significantly improved.

Showing how an open discussion about cultural beliefs can positively affect treatment.

<u>Griner and Smith (2006):</u>

A meta-analysis of 76 studies with a qualitative section on their effectiveness was included.

Cultural adaptions ranged from familiarizing the therapist with the client's cultural to training staff to be culturally sensitive.

Results showed that there were moderately strong benefits to culturally adaptions.

Treatment was more effective if the therapist spoke in the native tongue compared to English.

The benefit was 4 times stronger for same race client groups than mixed-race groups.

In conclusion, cultural adaptions for a specific

group of clients is more effective than making a general cultural adaptation.

Source: https://www.thinkib.net/psychology/page/22503/culture-and-treatment

Finally, here's another two interesting and key studies for this book.

'Parker, Cheah & Roy (2001) studied two sets of depressed out-patients, both living in their home countries. The first group was Malaysian Chinese and the second group was Australian Caucasian. In both cases, they were asked what their primary symptom was which led to them seeking medical help. In addition, they were asked to complete a survey of both physiological and cognitive symptoms of depression – ranking each symptom with regard to intensity and distress. The results showed that 60% of the Chinese and only 13% of the Australians identified a somatic symptom as their reason for seeking help. Australians were more likely to identify mood or cognitive difficulties. However, when comparing the inventory of symptoms that they experience, there was no significant difference in the number of somatic symptoms between the two groups. The Chinese did, however, report a much lower rate of cognitive symptoms.

Kirmayer (2001) argues that cultures have "explanatory models" for disorders. His theory is that cultures create socially acceptable sets of symptoms

A GUIDE TO MENTAL HEALTH AND TREATMENT AROUND THE WORLD

for mental distress. Since cultures are continually evolving, especially in the era of globalization, these explanatory models may change. This change in explanatory models may account for a seeming "rise" in the disorder within a culture. In the case of Japan, depression used to be seen as a need for spiritual guidance and/or time with family. They did not see depression as a "disorder," but rather sadness was seen as a way of tightening one's bonds with family and the community. Sadness, grief and melancholy were accepted as inevitable parts of life. As Japan has become more Westernized, Western symptoms have depression have become more common.'

Source: https://www.thinkib.net/psychology/page/22478/sociocultural-approach-to-depression

CHAPTER 6: DEPRESSION AND MENTAL HEALTH IN ASIA

Moving onto our first exploration, in this chapter, we'll be examining how culture impacts mental health in terms of treatment and beliefs in Asia. Focusing on Japan and China.

Japan:

As you will see as we look in this chapter, the Japanese approach to mental health couldn't be more different from the western approach.

One of the reasons for this is because depression in Japan isn't seen as a mental health disorder.

As a result of in Japan, the depressed personality type is admired and aspired. Which is radically different from the west as in the west we frown upon the depressed personality and we certainly don't aspire to it.

Therefore, we must think about why is it aspired to. While I'll fully admit that my research didn't find a reason why. One reason that could explain this admiration I'll explain in a moment after we look at mental health in Japan in more depth.

In Japanese culture, sadness, grief and depression are seen as well as accepted as an everyday part of life.

Moreover, based on Buddhist traditions, personal difficulties and by extension depression is seen as character building.

Consequently, could this admiration towards the depressed personality type be as a result of people seeing depression as the ultimate way to build character and people aspire to be depressed so that they can go on this unique character-building journey, to come out with a strong character?

It's logical reasoning.

Another unique or different approach to mental health in Japan compared to the west is that historically suicide isn't linked to mental health.

Due to in Japanese culture suicide has a tradition that is linked to honour as well as dedication.

A GUIDE TO MENTAL HEALTH AND TREATMENT AROUND THE WORLD

Many historical Japanese figures have performed suicide to avoid bringing shame or dishonour to their families, with the thinking being that if they die; the 'dishonourable' member of the family; then with the dead then honour is restored to the family. Like how honour killing work in the middle east or western crime families.

Examples of Japanese figures performing suicide are Samurai warriors and kamikaze pilots.

Although, the most interesting piece of this is that Japanese therapists, psychologists and psychiatrists don't see a link between suicide and mental health.

Nevertheless, Japan is starting to change very slowly to become more westernised because if you compare depression symptoms before and after westernisation then you would find that after westernisation depression symptoms are becoming like the symptoms of depression that show up in western cultures.

As symptoms for disorders do differ sometimes a lot between cultures.

Additionally, here are some surprising statistics about mental health in Japan.

- 6.6% of the population has met the standards for western cultures to state that the Japanese have depression.
- Japan has 26 suicide a year per 100,000 people. Compared to only 13 suicides per year per 100,000 in the USA.
- Prozac; an antidepressant; sells well in Japan but not as much as in other countries in the world.
- A Ministry of Health survey demonstrates that there's an increase in the number of children accessing mental health services. From 95,000 in 2002 to 148,000 in 2008.

Overall, suggesting that Japan does have a mental health problem as shown by its high suicide rate and the fact that Prozac sells well in Japan. Suggesting that a high number of people are taking in to deal with everyday life.

On the other hand, it's selling better in other countries suggesting that Japan has less of a mental health problem than other countries or more people prefer eastern methods of treatment compared to the west.

Returning to the point raised in the previous chapter about there are exceptions to the statement that there's a lack of reliable studies to examine the effectiveness of indigenous therapy.

A GUIDE TO MENTAL HEALTH AND TREATMENT AROUND THE WORLD

Morita therapy is a therapy that is rooted in the fundamental beliefs as well as values of the Japanese culture. These values and beliefs include:

- Emotions are natural responses to our life circumstances, and humans don't need to try to "fix" or "change" them.
- Dogmatic thinking- this thinking is that perfectionism in conjunction with high demands of the self, inhibit recovery and only when we are liberated from self-centeredness can we recover.
- In recovery, it's essential that are we left alone and resting instead of talking about our problems.

This type of Japanese therapy typically begins with a rest period before counselling begins. Although compared to counselling in the west, this counselling focuses on changing one's view toward the larger community instead of the self.

The therapy asks the patient to practise mindfulness through meditation as well.

Finally, the focus of the therapy is healing, not the origins of the disorder.

Applying This to Western Treatment:

Backing away from the theory, we can start to see the differences between this Japanese approach to treatment and the western methods of treatment.

As a result of in the west; at least in my experience; we don't believe or focus on mindfulness but in Japan, they believe that mindfulness is essential to recovery.

Another key difference between the western and Japanese approach is that in western treatment we focus on the origins of the disorder. Such as we focus on the biological, cognitive or social factors that could have caused the disorder. One way of doing this could be identifying any bad relationships in your life that could be causing your depression and encouraging you to change these relationships to become more positive or getting rid of these negative relationships completely.

Whereas the Japanese approach focuses on healing and moving on from the disorder.

Both I believe has its merits and drawbacks. For example, the western approach is good as it focuses on the causes of the disorder so these causes can be removed as a way towards recovery.

However, this method can seem a little too focused on negative and why as well as it could take a very, very long time to find all the factors or causes of depression in a person's life.

On the other hand, the Japanese approach is good because it focuses on recovery so the patient can focus on moving and improving without having to spend hours dissecting painful parts of their life searching for things that could be causing depression.

A GUIDE TO MENTAL HEALTH AND TREATMENT AROUND THE WORLD

Although the Japanese approach could be negative as it doesn't focus on the causes of the disorder and if these factors that are causing depression; like bad relationships, abuse and drug problems; are still in the person's life then there's a high chance of a relapse into depression.

Consequently, is it possible that the Japanese approach could be used to inform western treatment and improve it?

I strongly believe the answer is yes- because the Japanese approach works for Japan and its citizens. Therefore, I believe that if the western and Japanese approach hybridized to form a new type of treatment. Where the therapy focuses on origins and recovery then western treatment could be improved as we are focusing on the positive of recovery while finding the causes of depression and getting rid of them as well.

A study supporting the effectiveness of Japanese treatment is outlined below:

Ando et al (2009)

Researchers wanted to investigate the effect of mindfulness-based meditation therapy on Japanese patients who were suffering from anxiety and depression.

In total there were 28 patients that participated in two sessions of the therapy.

The patients were instructed to practice at home in-between sessions. The study used a pre-test / post-test design.

The patients completed questionnaires before as well as after the treatment.

Results showed that anxiety and depression levels decreased significantly. The researchers argue that a sense of spiritual wellbeing is what resulted in lower levels of both anxiety and depression.

Overall, supporting the idea that the Japanese approach that focuses on mindfulness is an effective treatment.

China:

China is another country of interest when it comes to mental health because China has its own classification system for health disorders as discussed in chapter 1 and inside the classification system that are many disorders that are unique to Chinese culture.

Such as Pa-Leng which is an extreme fear of the cold. This disorder seems to be unique to China as well as there are many other disorders that are unique to certain cultures. Hence, empathising the power of culture in mental health.

However, another reason China is of interest to this book is as a result of the mental health strain that is experienced by a lot of the Chinese population as it's suicide rate is reasonably high at 22.23 people per

A GUIDE TO MENTAL HEALTH AND TREATMENT AROUND THE WORLD

100,00 because of the poor working conditions and other factors. Especially, with their being famous cases of mass suicides at Apple's Chinese Manufacture FOXCONN.

Source: www.asiaone.com/health/chinas-suicide-rate-among-highest-world *and* www.telegraph.co.uk

Referring Back to Indigenous Therapies:

Another integral part of indigenous therapies is spirituality or religious practices.

For instance: as part of the therapy in Malaysia some of the techniques include: setting aside time for pray and focusing on verses of the Koran that focus on "worry"

Whereas, with Chinese patients verses from Taoist writings that focus on the following main principles: restricting selfish desires, learning how to be content, and learning to let go, are read by the patient followed by a reflection.

This approach is known as Chinese Taoist cognitive psychotherapy (CTCP).

Zhang et al (2002)

Researchers carried out a study to test the effectiveness of CTCP.

In their study, 143 Chinese patients with

Generalized Anxiety Disorder (GAD) were randomly assigned to one of three treatment groups: CTCP only, anti-anxiety drugs only, or a combination of the two.

The patients were evaluated before the study then after one month of their treatment and then again after six months of treatment.

Results showed that people on the anti-depressants showed better results than the CTCP group after one month.

Nevertheless, after six months those patients in the CTCP group had a greater reduction of symptoms.

Finally, people in the combined treatment group had the greatest symptom reduction with a low chance of relapse.

Overall, the researchers found that CTCP helped patients to reduce perfectionism as well as improve their coping skills. While the treatment was slower, the treatment appears to be more successful than drug treatment.

The results of this study are supported by other western studies that show that psychotherapy can be more effective in the long term for treating depression.

A GUIDE TO MENTAL HEALTH AND TREATMENT AROUND THE WORLD

Please refer to Abnormal Psychology for a more in-depth look at the effectiveness of psychotherapies for treating depression.

Barriers to Treatment:

This next section truly shows how culture can negatively impact treatment or rather the ability for people to get treatment as a result of cultural factors.

A report by Leong and Kalibatseva (2011) outlines the key barriers for Chinese Americans for getting treatment.

Cognitive Barriers:

This type of barrier refers to the way in which people think about treatment and this is influenced by their culture.

It's a common belief in several ethnic minorities such as Asian, Hispanic, and African Americans that a mental health problem can be treated or overcome through willpower and endurance of hardship without complaint. Instead of going to a profession for treatment.

Some research has indicated that Asian Americans are more likely than Caucasian Americans to believe that mental health was enhanced by exercising self-control.

Affective Barriers:

Many collectivistic cultures; cultures that tend to focus on the needs of the group instead of focusing on their own needs; avoid getting professional help in order to avoid the stigma as well as the shame of mental illness that is attached to mental health.

The main reason for this as we have previously mentioned in the Japanese section, it that the family's name is very important to collectivistic cultures and people don't want to bring shame or dishonour to their name because of their 'perceived weakness' or the fact that they are experiencing psychological difficulties and because of this people don't seek out professional help- so they can protect their family's reputation.

Sociocultural Barriers:

The report highlights many sociocultural barriers as well. For instance:

- Disclosing personal problems or family dysfunctions to a stranger. This is highly discouraged in collectivistic cultures.
- Lack of awareness or knowledge about available services.
- Mental health services could be unaffordable to people.
- Patients may not have time to receive care as they need to work multiple jobs or take care of family members.

A GUIDE TO MENTAL HEALTH AND TREATMENT AROUND THE WORLD

- Patients could have low English proficiency of immigrants
- There's a scarcity of bicultural and bilingual mental health professionals

Overall, Chinese culture has a massive impact on mental health from the increased strain on its citizens' mental health to its unique disorders. That I would encourage you to go and research for yourself. It's actually a fun activity to do.

In addition. The Chinese culture has a massive impact on treatment from china's specialized type of psychotherapy to the cultural barriers that prevent people from seeking professional help. It's futile to say that culture doesn't impact treatment.

CHAPTER 7: MENTAL HEALTH PRECEPTIONS EUROPE

Europe is an interesting continent I think because as modern and wealthy as Europe is. The continent is heavily divided because of many factors including politics, war, economics and trade.

<u>Eastern Europe:</u>

In addition, there's a mass gap between western Europe and Eastern Europe for a few reasons but the main reason being that in 1991 the Soviet Union fell leading to mass political change and unrest as well as economic devastation.

This led to the massive gap seen in today's Europe because while Western Europe continued to trade and get richer. The East was left to rebuild and even to this today eastern Europe hasn't managed to catch up to the rest of Europe.

Linking to Mental Health:

Recently research was performed that 'assessed the development of mental health services in 24 countries across the former Soviet Union and Eastern Bloc and the Southeast European countries over the last 25 years.'

Source: https://www.lshtm.ac.uk/newsevents/news/2018/mental-health-care-central-and-eastern-europe-remains-ineffective

The research area is of great interest because of the sheer amount of 'socio-economic and political changes have taken place since the fall of communism in CEE. However, after reviewing research on mental health services across the region the team showed that despite many promising policy documents, in practice mental health services are still reliant on large psychiatric hospitals with inadequate conditions. Many facilities are run-down and lacking in privacy.

The researchers found that underdevelopment of community care and lack of alternatives to hospital treatment in some countries led to unnecessary psychiatric admissions and long-term hospitalisations, in some cases for over 20 years. Stigma and discrimination against people with mental disorders were shown to be widespread, and human rights violations continue to occur.'

A GUIDE TO MENTAL HEALTH AND TREATMENT AROUND THE WORLD

Source: https://www.lshtm.ac.uk/newsevents/news/2018/mental-health-care-central-and-eastern-europe-remains-ineffective

The research shows that the culture surrounding mental health is one of stigma and discrimination. Which isn't surprising as if you think about it- western societies are only beginning to understand and destigmatising mental health disorders as we're becoming more modern and we have technology and science to show that mental health disorders aren't a problem that you can just deal with alone.

Therefore, it's not surprising that these eastern European countries have the same opinions that we had 30 years old before we knew about mental health.

Furthermore, it just shows that culture can impact mental health treatment in all countries even European countries as European is thought to be a modern revolutionary continent.

The research even shows that human rights are being broken which probably involves the mental health patients being put through some very unethical treatment or being treated as less than human.

In the exact same way that the United Kingdom and the USA treated mental health disorders in the

1800-1900s with waterboarding and electroshock therapy.

Overall, it demonstrates how the eastern European culture surrounding mental health and the culture that demonises mental health has negatively impacted treatment as the culture has left to ineffective and possibly unethical treatments being performed. Instead of more helping and humane treatment being used.

'The research highlights the need for mental health to be recognised as a public health priority and to be allocated resources that are proportional to the burden of these conditions. CEE countries apportion an estimated 3% of their health care budgets to mental health (equivalent to US$18.70 per person), which is far below the average in EU countries outside of the former eastern bloc, with an average of 7% (equivalent to US$293.70 per person). The team found a lack of economic evaluations and epidemiological evidence to support the allocation of these scarce resources.

Mental health legislation has been passed and introduced in several CEE countries. However, in many countries, this was mostly due to external pressures in order to meet EU standards, rather than as a result of genuine attempts to modernise the services. In Albania and Kosovo, for example, the mental health legislation remains largely unimplemented, services underfunded, and stigma still very high."

Source: https://www.lshtm.ac.uk/newsevents/news/2018/mental-health-care-central-and-eastern-europe-remains-ineffective

The two paragraphs above further demonstrate the eastern European culture towards mental health as it shows that mental health is not a priority as supported by its minimal spending on mental health resources, and the findings that the research team has found no evidence to explain why the countries do not spend money on mental health; for example: a war could possibly explain why these countries refuse to put more money into mental health; this further proves that as a result of their cultural beliefs towards mental health they refuse to invest in mental health services.

Moreover, the last paragraph shows that the only reason why there is mental health legalisation or services in the first place is as a result of a need to meet EU standards as well as pressures from external sources, is another example of how culture can impact mental health.

Italy:

Italy a great country in my opinion.

Great history, great culture and most importantly great food.

However, when I came across this research study I was a bit surprised because the study below is a national survey involving 1001 Italian people's views towards mental health and I thought that with Italy being a modern country that their views would be more open-minded about depression.

I'll explain more as we explore this section.

The results of the research study were:

- 98% of people were aware of depression
- 62% had experienced depression
- 75% believed that people that suffered from depression shouldn't talk about their problem.
- A minority believed that depression should be managed without external help. Basically, it's your problem so you need to deal with it.
- Among perceived causes of depression, most respondents mentioned life stressors or physical strains.
- Psychologists were often indicated as an adequate source of professional help.

A GUIDE TO MENTAL HEALTH AND TREATMENT AROUND THE WORLD

- Half of the sample believed that depression should be pharmacologically treated, but drugs were often seen as addictive.
- Many people thought that doctors are too busy to treat patients suffering from depression.

Source: Carmine Munizza, Piergiorgio Argentero, Alessandro Coppo, Giuseppe Tibaldi, Massimo Di Giannantonio, Rocco Luigi Picci, and Paola Rucci, Public Beliefs and Attitudes towards Depression in Italy: A National Survey, PloS ONE 2013

Personally, I find these results interesting because it shows the common results in a modern country because you have the thinking of an educated society as supported by among perceived causes of depression, most respondents mentioned life stressors or physical strains and 98% people were aware of depression. Demonstrating that Italian society like other western societies are not ignorance or at least not completely ignorant about what causes depression.

However, I am surprised that Italian society and no doubt other members of western societies believe that help who suffer from mental health disorders shouldn't talk about their problems, as without talking about the problem how can things improve?

Additionally, this is something that I love about culture and the west because in my experience western culture teaches us or tries to make us believe that we are the best culture and that we are smarter than other cultures, but what we don't teach ourselves is that we have our faults in perceived intelligence as we still hold old fashioned beliefs that aren't true. Such as homosexuality is wrong, and citizens of western societies read hundreds of pieces of information each day and some of it is probably false. As a result of fake news and people just writing opinions and labelling them facts.

Overall, this study demonstrates that even modern societies and their cultural beliefs can negatively impact mental health as in this case the Italian culture has a widespread belief that mental health sufferers shouldn't talk about their problems.

Finally, I believe that the conclusion below perfectly summarises western societies' beliefs and attuites towards mental health.

<u>'Conclusions</u>

Our findings indicate that depression is seen as a reaction to significant life events that should be overcome with the support of significant others or the help of health professionals (mainly psychologists). However, there are still barriers to the disclosure of depressive symptoms to PCPs, and concerns about the addictive effect of antidepressants. In the presence of a gap between people's beliefs and what health professionals consider appropriate for the treatment of depression, a "shared decision making" approach to treatment selection should be adopted taking into account the patients' preference for psychological interventions to ensure active compliance with effective treatments.'

Source: Carmine Munizza, Piergiorgio Argentero, Alessandro Coppo, Giuseppe Tibaldi, Massimo Di Giannantonio, Rocco Luigi Picci, and Paola Rucci, Public Beliefs and Attitudes towards Depression in Italy: A National Survey, PloS ONE 2013

CHAPTER 8: PRECEPTIONS AND COSTS OF DEPRESSION IN AFRICA

Africa- one of the poorest continents in the world.

Yet it's equally an amazing continent in my opinion filled with wonders from ancient civilisations. Like: ancient. As well as filled with beautiful landscapes and wildlife.

In addition, it's filled with impressive people that in a way have knowledge and experience that is dying out in today's world as they can live and thrive without technology and many aspects of daily life that we western civilisation take for granted.

Nevertheless, while Africa is a wondrous place, 25% African women are suffering from depression and in that 25% of people. 85% of them have no access to treatment.

Below is a list of facts as well as statistics for

depression in Africa.

Source: https://strongminds.org/why-depression-in-africa/

Personal Well-being

Uganda- depression was significantly negatively correlated with literacy rates.

Uganda- elevated depression scores were associated with females having a higher number of sexual partners.

Ghana and Uganda- depression impairs rural's women's abilities to farm, cook and grow food.

Treatment Acess:

Ghana- only 1.2% of depressed individuals receive the required treatment.

Nigeria- depressed elderly people with low economic status and/or rural residence received no treatment for depression during lifetime.

Nigeria-more than 50% of people with depression reported that their social role was moderately impaired.

A GUIDE TO MENTAL HEALTH AND TREATMENT AROUND THE WORLD

Physical Health

Sub-Saharan Africa- people with depression have a 300% increased chance of getting migraines.

Nigeria, Uganda and South Africa- the prevalence of depression in HIV infected populations varies widely from 29% in Nigeria, 39% in South Africa and up to 54% in Uganda.

Economic Productivity:

Nigeria- 83% of people with depression reported that their work-related activities were moderately impaired with 60% being severely impaired.

Uganda-amongst people with HIV and major depression, depression alleviation was associated with a nearly a doubling of weekly hours worked.

South Africa- $4,798 was the average lost income for people diagnosed with depression each year.

Child Impact:

Nigeria- depressed mothers are more likely to stop breast feeding their infants early. This contributes to poor nutrition and poor immunity for infants.

Also, infants in Nigeria with depressed mothers have lower growth rates and more common diarrhea and infection than infants with non-depressed mothers.

Similar results have been found in Malawi.

Household Functioning:

In Nigeria, 76% of depressed people said their home activites were moderately impacired and 12% said it was severely impaired.

In Burkina Faso, depression was positively corrlated with living in a household with low food security.

Finally, in South Africa, maternal depression decreases families' economic security because fo the days lost at work.

From The Data:

As we have witnessed in this data, we can clearly see that depression in Africa and no doubt the rest of the world has very real and very damaging consequences.

As in the box above, we can clearly see that in Nigeria the country's productivity is impaired because of depression.

Putting this impact in a real-world context this is damaging for serval reasons. For example:

- It decreases the number of goods the country can produce.
- Resulting in a decrease in the number of products the country can trade with.
- Equalling a possible loss of revenue for the country.
- To reinvest in itself so the country can grow and develop.
- Ultimately leading to the stagnation for the country's development and a possible increase in poverty.

Therefore, this further supports the idea that is neglected around the world that mental health does have real-world impacts.

<u>Focus on Uganda:</u>

In this section, we'll be analysing the results of an analysis of 4 academic papers on how the Baganda people in Uganda see depression as a result of their cultural beliefs.

Yet first I'll give you a bit of context- some facts include:

Population: roughly 3 million

Language: Luganda

Religion: Christianity and Islam

The Baganda people are a group of people that live in the subkingdom of Baganda that is a part of Uganda. Traditionally, the kingdom was ruled by a king that had complete control of it's social, political and all other matters, but after the subkingdom's abolishment in 1967 and then the reinstatement of the kingdoms in 1993. The King only has ritual power and no political power.

Source: https://www.everyculture.com/wc/Tajikistan-to-Zimbabwe/Baganda.html

Furthermore, this culture is a collectivistic culture meaning that they focus on the needs of the group compared to their individual needs.

Now that you know more about the culture and most importantly that it's a collectivist culture. We can start to move onto analysing the results.

Analyse of the results of 'Stockholm and Kampala, 2006, Cultural explanatory models of depression in Uganda, Karolinska Institutet'

Firstly, depression is largely regarded by the Baganda people as clan illnesses. As supported by: 'depression with psychotic features was regarded as a 'clan illness' arising from a poor relationships with the living and the dead' (Elialiia Sarikiaeli Okello, 2006) this suggests that in the culture of the Baganda depression is seen as illness that can impact the village, as well as their cultural beliefs, tend to focus on the social reasons for depression. As whilst the reasoning in the quote above is a little superstition, if you peel back the layers to reveal the true meaning of the quote then you can see that the culture is saying that depression arises from a poor relationship with people in their lives; which is supported by research; as well as a bad relationship with the dead. For example: if their mother died before the person could apologise for any mistakes in life.

In addition, the Baganda people are opposed to western influence and treatment. As supported by: 'Both illnesses were perceived as not requiring western medication but culturally accepted corrective traditional therapies' (Elialiia Sarikiaeli Okello, 2006) overall, suggesting that the Baganda people are wary of western medication. This could be for several reasons such as: not understanding why the medication was needed, thinking that their therapies were the best course of treatment as well as there could have been religious or superstition reasons. Nevertheless, in terms of treatment this demonstrates that the Baganda approach to depression is different to the west as they prefer their cultural therapies whereas the west prefers to use medication.

Finally, depending on how socially disruptive the

person determines if they go into psychiatric care. As supported by: 'particularly those defined as socially disruptive, were important determinants of entry to psychiatric care'(Elialiia Sarikiaeli Okello, 2006) therefore, this suggests that in their culture they believe that if a person isn't socially disruptive then they shouldn't seek professional help because they aren't a problem to their society. Furthermore, the paper later states 'non-disruptive symptoms were often ignored, misdiagnosed or treated as a physical problem' (Elialiia Sarikiaeli Okello, 2006) consequently, showing that in their culture mental health isn't picked up or 'believed in' to some extent unless it causes a disruption to society.

CONCLUSION

I will keep this conclusion and a bit informal as we are now at the end of our cultural journey.

In conclusion, culture can impact how depression is perceived and treated by the people of a given culture in a number of different ways and this is present in all cultures because all cultures perceive depression in different ways. Furthermore, this perception of depression can possible negatively impact treatment but not always.

Some cultural variations in the perception of depression include:

- Japanese professionals do not see a link between suicide and mental health whereas in western societies we would see a very strong link between suicide and mental health.
- Japanese people admire and aspire to the depressed personality type whereas the west prefers to shunt or even 'fear' the depressed personality type.
- The Baganda people do not see the need to treat depression with medication but instead,

they believe that their own types of indigenous psychotherapies are the best course of treatment. Whereas in the west as we follow the biomedical model; a model where we believe that depression and many disorders can as a result of biological problems; we believe that we can fix the problems with medication and sometimes social factors and psychological factors are overlooked or not considered at all.

As you can see in the world there is a lot of cultural variations in terms of perception and attitudes towards depression as well as treatment.

Overall, the point of this book is to open your eyes to the different ideas around the world about depression and to show you that culture has a massive impact on people's beliefs about depression as well as how depression is treated around the world.

I hope you've found this as interesting as I have…

A GUIDE TO MENTAL HEALTH AND TREATMENT AROUND THE WORLD

Bibliography:

Whiteley, C. (2019) Abnormal Psychology First Edition. CGD Publishing. (New Edition Available)

https://www.thinkib.net/psychology/page/27585/presentation-sociocultural-and-mdd

First accessed on 15th August 2019

https://www.thinkib.net/psychology/page/22478/sociocultural-approach-to-depression

First accessed on 15th August 2019

https://www.thinkib.net/psychology/page/22503/culture-and-treatment

First accessed on 15th August 2019

www.asiaone.com/health/chinas-suicide-rate-among-highest-world

First accessed on 15th August 2019

www.telegraph.co.uk

First accessed on 15th August 2019

https://www.ncbi.nlm.nih.gov/pmc/articles/PMC3659050/

First accessed on 15th August 2019

Carmine Munizza, Piergiorgio Argentero, Alessandro Coppo, Giuseppe Tibaldi, Massimo Di Giannantonio, Rocco Luigi Picci, and Paola Rucci, Public Beliefs and Attitudes towards Depression in Italy: A National Survey, PloS ONE 2013

https://www.lshtm.ac.uk/newsevents/news/2018/mental-health-care-central-and-eastern-europe-remains-ineffective

First accessed on 15th August 2019

https://strongminds.org/why-depression-in-africa/

First accessed on 15th August 2019

Elialilia Sarikiaeli Okello, Karolinska Institutet, Cultural Explanatory models of depression in Uganda, 2006

Lee Parker (author), Darren Seath (author) Alexey Popov (author), *Oxford IB Diploma Programme: Psychology Course Companion,* 2nd edition, OUP Oxford, 2017

Alexey Popov, *IB Psychology Study Guide: Oxford IB Diploma Programme,* 2nd edition, OUP Oxford, 2018

https://www.medicalnewstoday.com/kc/serotonin-facts-232248

first accessed on 18th March 2019

A GUIDE TO MENTAL HEALTH AND TREATMENT AROUND THE WORLD

https://www.thinkib.net/psychology/page/22460/biological-approach-to-depression

First accessed on 18th March 2019

https://www.subscribepage.com/psychologyboxset

A GUIDE TO MENTAL HEALTH AND TREATMENT AROUND THE WORLD

Thank you for reading.

I hoped you enjoyed it.

If you want a FREE book and keep up to date about new books and project. Then please sign up for my newsletter at www.connorwhiteley.net/

Have a great day.

CHECK OUT THE PSYCHOLOGY WORLD PODCAST FOR MORE PSYCHOLOGY INFORMATION!

AVAILABLE ON ALL MAJOR PODCAST APPS.

About the author:

Connor Whiteley is the author of over 30 books in the sci-fi fantasy, nonfiction psychology and books for writer's genre and he is a Human Branding Speaker and Consultant.

He is a passionate warhammer 40,000 reader, psychology student and author.

Who narrates his own audiobooks and he hosts The Psychology World Podcast.

All whilst studying Psychology at the University of Kent, England.

Also, he was a former Explorer Scout where he gave a speech to the Maltese President in August 2018 and he attended Prince Charles' 70th Birthday Party at Buckingham Palace in May 2018.

Plus, he is a self-confessed coffee lover!

A GUIDE TO MENTAL HEALTH AND TREATMENT AROUND THE WORLD

Please follow me on:

Website: www.connorwhiteley.net

Twitter: @scifiwhiteley

Please leave on honest review as this helps with the discoverability of the book and I truly appreciate it.

Thank you for reading. I hope you've enjoyed.

All books in 'An Introductory Series':

BIOLOGICAL PSYCHOLOGY 3RD EDITION

COGNITIVE PSYCHOLOGY 2ND EDITION

SOCIAL PSYCHOLOGY- 3RD EDITION

ABNORMAL PSYCHOLOGY 3RD EDITION

PSYCHOLOGY OF RELATIONSHIPS- 3RD EDITION

DEVELOPMENTAL PSYCHOLOGY 3RD EDITION

HEALTH PSYCHOLOGY

RESEARCH IN PSYCHOLOGY

A GUIDE TO MENTAL HEALTH AND TREATMENT AROUND THE WORLD- A GLOBAL LOOK AT DEPRESSION

FORENSIC PSYCHOLOGY

THE FORENSIC PSYCHOLOGY OF THEFT, BURGLARY AND OTHER RIMES AGAINST PROPERTY

CRIMINAL PROFILING: A FORENSIC PSYCHOLOGY GUIDE TO FBI PROFILING AND GEOGRAPHICAL AND STATISTICAL PROFILING.

A GUIDE TO MENTAL HEALTH AND TREATMENT AROUND THE WORLD

CLINICAL PSYCHOLOGY

FORMULATION IN PSYCHOTHERAPY

Companion guides:

BIOLOGICAL PSYCHOLOGY 2ND EDITION WORKBOOK

COGNITIVE PSYCHOLOGY 2ND EDITION WORKBOOK

SOCIOCULTURAL PSYCHOLOGY 2ND EDITION WORKBOOK

ABNORMAL PSYCHOLOGY 2ND EDITION WORKBOOK

PSYCHOLOGY OF HUMAN RELATIONSHIPS 2ND EDITION WORKBOOK

HEALTH PSYCHOLOGY WORKBOOK

FORENSIC PSYCHOLOGY WORKBOOK

OTHER SHORT STORIES BY CONNOR WHITELEY

Blade of The Emperor

Arbiter's Truth

The Bloodied Rose

Asmodia's Wrath

Other books by Connor Whiteley:

THE ANGEL OF RETURN

THE ANGEL OF FREEDOM

GARRO: GALAXY'S END

GARRO: RISE OF THE ORDER

GARRO: END TIMES

GARRO: SHORT STORIES

GARRO: COLLECTION

GARRO: HERESY

GARRO: FAITHLESS

GARRO: DESTROYER OF WORLDS

GARRO: COLLECTIONS BOOK 4-6

GARRO: MISTRESS OF BLOOD

A GUIDE TO MENTAL HEALTH AND TREATMENT AROUND THE WORLD

GARRO: BEACON OF HOPE

GARRO: END OF DAYS

WINTER'S COMING

WINTER'S HUNT

WINTER'S REVENGE

WINTER'S DISSENSION

Audiobooks by Connor Whiteley:

BIOLOGICAL PSYCHOLOGY

COGNITIVE PSYCHOLOGY

SOCIOCULTURAL PSYCHOLOGY

ABNORMAL PSYCHOLOGY

PSYCHOLOGY OF HUMAN RELATIONSHIPS

HEALTH PSYCHOLOGY

DEVELOPMENTAL PSYCHOLOGY

RESEARCH IN PSYCHOLOGY

FORENSIC PSYCHOLOGY

GARRO: GALAXY'S END

GARRO: RISE OF THE ORDER

GARRO: SHORT STORIES

GARRO: END TIMES

GARRO: COLLECTION

GARRO: HERESY

GARRO: FAITHLESS

GARRO: DESTROYER OF WORLDS

A GUIDE TO MENTAL HEALTH AND TREATMENT AROUND THE WORLD

GARRO: COLLECTION BOOKS 4-6

GARRO: COLLECTION BOOKS 1-6

Business books:

TIME MANAGEMENT: A GUIDE FOR STUDENTS AND WORKERS

LEADERSHIP: WHAT MAKES A GOOD LEADER? A GUIDE FOR STUDENTS AND WORKERS.

BUSINESS SKILLS: HOW TO SURVIVE THE BUSINESS WORLD? A GUIDE FOR STUDENTS, EMPLOYEES AND EMPLOYERS.

BUSINESS COLLECTION

GET YOUR FREE BOOK AT:
WWW.CONNORWHITELEY.NET

www.ingramcontent.com/pod-product-compliance
Lightning Source LLC
LaVergne TN
LVHW011853060526
838200LV00054B/4298